·DON'TS·
FOR
HUSBANDS

19 13

·DON'TS·
FOR
WIVES

BY

BLANCHE EBBUTT

LONDON
A. & C. BLACK, LTD.
1913

CONTENTS

DON'TS FOR HUSBANDS

DON'TS FOR WIVES

DON'TS
FOR HUSBANDS

PREFACE

You are neither as bad nor as good a fellow as you imagine yourself to be. No doubt you know a good deal about women, but (if you are in the early years of your married life) not nearly as much as you will in another decade. In any case I hope that, when you have read my little book, you will thank me for having told you many things that otherwise you could have learned only by experience, more or less bitter according to

1

the discretion exercised both by you and by your other half.

Women, married or single, are kittle-cattle; and, as for men—well, I have a husband myself!

BLANCHE EBBUTT.

DON'TS FOR HUSBANDS

I.—GENERAL HABITS.

DON'T drop cigarette ash all over the drawing-room carpet. Some people will tell you that it improves the colours, but your wife won't care to try that recipe.

Don't throw cigar-ends into the bowl of water your wife keeps in front of the gas-fire. They are not ornamental, and she will not be pleased.

Don't increase the necessary work of the house by leaving all your things lying about in different places. If

3

you are not tidy by nature, at least be thoughtful for others.

Don't sit down to breakfast in your shirt-sleeves in hot weather on the ground that "only your wife" is present. She is a woman like any other woman. The courtesies you give to womankind are her due, and she will appreciate them.

Don't take it out on your poor wife every time you have a headache or a cold. It isn't her fault, and she has enough to do in nursing you, without having to put up with ill-humour into the bargain.

Don't flourish a grimy handkerchief about because you have forgotten to take a clean one out of your box or your drawer. If your wife provides you with a reasonable stock, you might at least take the trouble to remember to use them.

Don't stoop, even if your work is desk-work. Your wife wants to see you straight and broad-chested.

Don't slouch. No one who cares for a man likes to see him acquire a slouching habit.

Don't be too grave and solemn. Raise a bit of fun in the home now and then.

Don't keep all your best jokes for your men friends. Let your wife share them.

Don't look at things solely from a man's point of view. Put yourself in your wife's place and see how you would like some of the things she has to put up with.

Don't fidget. Some husbands are never still for a moment. They walk in and out of rooms like the wandering Jew; they play with the salt at dinner; they draw lines on the tablecloth with a fork; they tap the table with their fingers and the floor with their feet; they creak their slippers and drop the coal tongs on to the tiled hearth. In fact, they keep their wives in a state of tension, and the poor creatures would need nerves of iron to enable them to stand the strain.

Don't make a fuss when your wife has "unattached" women friends to be seen home at night. I have seen men on these occasions look at their slippers, and fuss about changing into walking-shoes, and look out to see whether it rains, etc., until I should certainly have gone off alone had I been the guest to be escorted.

Don't sharpen pencils all over the house as you walk about. Try a hearth or a waste-paper basket, or a news-paper. It does not improve either carpets or the servants' temper to find scraps of pencil-sharpenings all over the floors.

Don't delegate the carving to your wife on the plea that you "can't" carve. You should be ashamed to own that you can't do a little thing like that as well as a woman can. It is just laziness on your part. Besides, a man ought to take the head of his own table.

Don't always refuse to go shopping with your wife. Of course it's a nuisance, but sometimes she honestly wants your advice, and you ought to be pleased to give it.

Don't be conceited about your good looks. It is more than probable that no one but yourself is aware of them ; anyway, you are not responsible for them, and vanity in a man is ridiculous.

Don't refuse to get up and investigate in the night if your wife hears an unusual noise, or fancies she smells fire or escaping gas. She will be afraid of shaming you by getting up herself, and will lie awake working herself into a fever. This may be illogical, but it's true.

Don't hang about the house all day if your occupation does not take you abroad. Spend regular hours in your study or "den," or go out and play golf; but don't inflict your company on your wife during every minute of every day. She is fond of you, but she wants to be free sometimes. And *she* has business to do, if you haven't.

II.—PERSONAL RELATIONS.

Don't keep up the "poor little woman" pose too long. A woman may like to be a plaything for a little while, but the novelty soon wears off.

Don't condescend; you are not the only person in the house with brains.

Don't be surprised, or annoyed, or disappointed, to find, after treating your wife for years as a feather-brain, that you have made her one, and that she fails to rise to the occasion when you need her help.

Don't keep her in cotton-wool. She isn't wax—she's a woman.

Don't try to take all work and worry off her shoulders. You can't attend to her business and your own too.

Don't shelter her from every wind that blows. You will kill her soul that way, if you save her body.

Don't forget that you are not immortal. What chance will she have if you die and leave her with no knowledge of the ways of the wicked world?

Don't omit to bring home an occasional bunch of flowers or a few chocolates. Your wife will value even a penny bunch of violets for your thought of her.

Don't rush out of the house in such a hurry that you haven't time to kiss your wife "good-bye." She will grieve over the omission all day.

Don't belittle your wife before visitors. You may think it a joke to speak of her little foibles, but she will not easily forgive you.

Don't be careless about keeping promises made to your wife. If you have promised to be at home at seven, think twice before you go off with a friend at 6.30.

Don't hesitate to mention the fact when you think your wife looks especially nice. Your thinking so can give her no pleasure unless you tell your thought.

Don't forget your wife's birthday. Even if she doesn't want the whole world to know her age, she doesn't like *you* to forget.

Don't think that because you can't afford to buy an expensive present, it is best to take no notice at all. The smallest gift will be appreciated if prompted by love.

Don't sulk when things go wrong. If you can't help being vexed, say so, and get it over.

Don't "nag" your wife. If she *has* burnt the cake or forgotten to sew on a button, she doesn't want to be told of it over and over again.

Don't shout when you are angry. It isn't necessary to let the children or the servants know all about it.

Don't scowl or look severe. Cultivate a pleasant expression if Nature hasn't blessed you with one.

Don't "let off steam" on your wife or children every time anything goes wrong in the garage or the garden, or the fowl-house, or the dark room.

Try to realise that they have nothing to do with it, and that it is unfair to make them suffer for it.

Don't allow yourself to become selfish. It is so easy, because wives are mostly ready to give way. Watch yourself, and if you find that you always tend to appropriate the most comfortable chair, or the warmest corner, or the most interesting book, just check the habit.

Don't quarrel with your wife. She can't, if you won't. Mud sticks, and so do words spoken in anger.

Don't refuse your wife's overtures when next you meet if you *have* unfortunately had a bit of a breeze. Remember it costs her something to make them, and if you weren't a bit of a pig, you would save her the embarrassment by making them yourself.

Don't ever tell your wife a lie about anything. There should be entire confidence between you. If she once finds you out in a lie, she will not believe you when you *do* speak the truth.

Don't "talk down" to your wife. She has as much intelligence as your colleague at the office; she lacks only opportunity. Talk to her (explaining when necessary) of anything you would talk of to a man, and you will be surprised to find how she expands.

Don't think that it is no longer necessary to *show* your love for your wife, as she "ought to know it by this time." A woman likes to be kissed and caressed and to receive little lover-like attentions from her husband even when she is a grandmother.

Don't expect happiness if you married for money; once she realises it, your wife won't let you forget it.

Don't think that if you married merely to get an unpaid housekeeper that position is going to satisfy your wife. She could have obtained a good salary as professional housekeeper to any other man if she had wanted to: she married for other reasons.

Don't think that because you and your wife married for love there will never be a cloud in your sky. Neither of you is perfect, and you will have to learn to avoid treading on each other's corns.

Don't expect your wife to do all the cheering up while you do all the giving way when things go wrong. Share and share alike.

Don't dwell on any lack of physical perfection in your wife. Beauty of mind is much more important than beauty of body.

Don't despise your wife's everyday qualities because she is not what the world would call brilliant. Sound common sense is of more value than fireworks when one is running a home.

Don't call your wife a coward because she is afraid of a spider. Probably in a case of real danger she would prove to be quite as brave as you.

Don't be irritated now by the childish ways in your wife that amused you so much in your *fiancée*. She will grow out of them soon enough.

Don't put on too much of the "lord of creation" air. It will only make you look ridiculous.

Don't think that, because she is a woman, your wife ought to be an angel of light. She is just as much a human being as you are, and no more perfect.

Don't keep your wife outside your business interests. It is foolish to say that she knows nothing about the business, and therefore it can't interest her.

You will often find, too, that her fresh mind will see a way out of some little difficulty that has not occurred to you.

Don't worship your wife as a saint, and then when you discover that she is, after all, of common clay, spend the rest of your life mourning her deterioration. Probably she is what she always was, and it is only that you are looking at her through different glasses.

Don't take the attitude that wives, like children, should be seen and not heard. No doubt you are a very clever fellow, and it is an education for her to listen to you, but she also may have some views worth mentioning.

Don't expect to understand every detail of the working of your wife's mind. A woman arrives at things by different ways, and it is useless to worry her with "Why?" does she think this or that.

Don't try to keep bad news from your wife. She will guess that something is wrong, and will worry far more than if you tell her straight out.

Don't neglect seeing your wife off, or meeting her on her return from a journey, on the ground that she is so capable that she doesn't need you. Perhaps not, but she would like to see you, all the same.

Don't allow the habit of silence at home to grow upon you. Of course, you don't want to keep up polite conversation with an effort—that is not at all what I mean; but some husbands never seem to think it worth while to talk to their wives about anything, although if a friend comes in, they will at once begin an animated conversation.

Don't expect your wife to wait on you hand and foot. She is good for other things than to fetch and carry for you. If you don't exact it, it will give her pleasure to wait on you to a reasonable extent.

Don't think you can live your lives apart under the same roof and still be happy. Marriage is a joint affair, and cannot comfortably be worked along separate lines.

Don't insist upon having the last word. If you know when to drop an argument, you are a wise man.

Don't think it is undignified to give way where you and your wife think differently. If it is on a matter of principle, show her why you think as you do, and she will respect your reasons; but you must equally hear her reasons and respect them.

Don't try to regulate every detail of your wife's life. Even a wife is an individual, and must be allowed some scope.

Don't expect your wife to hold the same views as yours on every conceivable question. Some men like an echo, it is true, but it becomes very wearisome in time.

Don't hesitate to talk politics with your wife. Many men are satisfied to believe that "women don't understand politics." Why don't they? Because they never have a chance to crystallise their beliefs by thrashing out questions of public interest in argument with men who have studied them. Encourage your wife to read and talk of political matters. Never mind if she sees things quite differently from you; let her form her own views and express them.

Don't drop, when alone with your wife, the little courtesies you would offer to other women. For instance, always get up to open a door for her, as you would for a lady guest.

Don't fall into the habit of regarding your wife merely as the mother of your children. There is no need for her to cease to be your chum because she is a mother; but if she finds that you tend to relegate her to a back seat, she will gradually allow the children to absorb her more and more.

Don't drop calling her "Laura" or "Kiddie," and address her as "Mamma" or "Mother" in season and out of season. She is proud to be a mother, but she wants to be a wife too.

Don't try to "drive" your wife. You will find it so much easier to lead her.

Don't be "riled" by a bit of good-natured chaff from your wife. There is no bitterness in it, and she probably has to stand a good deal of the same sort of thing from you.

Don't fail to treat your wife with due respect. Let there be nothing of the high and mighty suggestion that a mere woman can't possibly understand things. There are even realms in which you can look up to her as owning superior knowledge, and there are none in which she is to be despised.

Don't begin your married life by expecting too much. If you expect little, you will be saved a good deal of disappointment.

Don't say it's a good thing to speak home truths now and again to your wife. It only means that you want to be nasty.

Don't forget to be your wife's best friend as well as her husband. True friendship in marriage does away with all sorts of trouble.

Don't expect a "return" for every generous action. It ceases to be generous if there be an *arrière pensée* in it.

Don't chide your wife in public, whatever you may feel it necessary to do in private. She will not easily forgive you for having witnesses to her discomfiture.

Don't be chary of your praise. Whether it be a new design for a dress, a more becoming style of hairdressing, or a "fetching" little entrée at dinner, give praise where praise is due. It will not only make your wife happier, but will even confirm your own good-humour; and good-humour is always worth cultivating for its own sake.

Don't forget that actions speak louder than words. It's no use telling your wife how much you care for her if you do the very things that you know will make her unhappy.

Don't flatter your wife. Unless she is very vain, she is sure to see through you, and she will be more hurt than pleased. Praise where you can, but leave flattery alone.

Don't assume that it is always your wife who is wrong whenever you have a difference of opinion. After all, you are not infallible.

Don't judge your wife's motives. She may do a thing from a motive that would never occur to you, and be perfectly justified in her action.

Don't be reserved with your wife, however natural it is to you to be reserved with others. Be perfectly open and confiding in all your dealings with her. She will be deeply hurt if she is left to discover for herself something that she had a right to expect you to tell her.

Don't let ambition crowd out love. There ought to be room for both in your life, but some men are so busy "getting on" that they have no time to make love to their wives.

Don't neglect to write daily to your wife when you are absent from each other. Even if you can manage only a few lines, it will show her that you are thinking about her.

Don't think you can soothe wounded feelings by material gifts. I knew a man who bought his wife a ring or a pendant to "make it up" every time he had been especially horrid to her, but it did not heal the breach. She would gladly have given all her jewellery to feel that her husband loved her too well to hurt her.

Don't start arguments about religion unless you and your wife can both discuss the matter quite impersonally. The bitterest quarrels sometimes arise from religious discussion. On the other hand—

Don't stifle discussion in your home. Let every member of the family contribute his ideas, and there will be none of the stagnation one so often meets in homes where discussion of any and every subject is prohibited.

Don't make fun of your wife if she happens to make a little mistake. She is probably very sensitive, and will get into the habit of withdrawing into her shell, so that you will lose much valuable intercourse that might have been yours.

Don't forget that it is the little things that count in married life. Avoid trivial jealousies; trivial selfishnesses; tiny irritants; small outbursts of temper; short sarcastic comments. If you can't say something pleasant, learn to keep silence.

III.—JEALOUSY.

Don't try to be a Sultan. This is the West; and you can't shut your wife away from other men. Don't insult her by trying to.

Don't tease your wife about every pretty girl you meet. She may not be jealous to begin with, but after a while she may begin to think that there is something in it.

Don't object to a servant on the score of her looks. You wife will take care not to engage a pretty maid if she suspects you of undue interest in her appearance.

Don't object to your wife going out with another man if you can't take her yourself—so long as you know and approve of the man.

Don't imagine your wife never wants to see any other man than you. However nice she thinks you, it is possible to have too much of a good thing.

Don't, if you think your wife sees too much of another man, forbid her to speak to him. You will perhaps only crystallise a wandering fancy by this method. Fill up her time yourself; take her out a good deal, and the too friendly attitude will soon die a natural death. But a woman of spirit won't be coerced.

Don't dwell on the beauty of other women if you know your wife to be sensitive on the point. There is no sense in rubbing sores, although some men seem to find a strange pleasure in it.

Don't be continually telling your wife what a charming woman Mrs. Jones is, or how lucky Brown is in having a wife who can cook such dainty dishes. You can't expect her to relish having the good qualities of these other wives rammed down her throat.

Don't throw your mother's perfections at her head, or you needn't be surprised if she suggests that you might as well return to your mother's wing. Remember that your mother was an experienced housekeeper before you were born, and that your wife is only just beginning.

Don't be jealous of your wife's girl friends. If she wants to spend the day with them now and then, spare her with a good grace. Don't let her feel that you are a selfish tyrant.

Don't give up all the friends of your bachelorhood. Ask them to your home, and your wife will make them welcome, whether men or women.

Don't flirt with other women. Your wife may or may not be jealous, but she will certainly despise you if you do.

Don't neglect your wife because your grown-up daughter is such a charming companion. She can be a good chum to you without usurping her mother's place in your affections.

Don't raise objections to your wife's work among the poor on the score that "charity begins at home." Quite true, but it needn't end there. It is mean of you to be jealous of the time a good woman spends in helping those less fortunate than herself.

Don't forget to trust your wife in everything—in money matters; in her relations with other men; in her correspondence. Trust her to the utmost, and you will rarely find your trust misplaced.

IV.—HINTS ON FINANCE.

Don't neglect to insure your life for a reasonable sum. Then you will at least know that your wife will not be left in actual want if you die suddenly.

Don't do all the ordering and all the paying yourself on the ground that your wife doesn't understand money matters. Let her learn to understand them.

Don't be niggardly about the household supplies if you can afford to be generous. You can't make omelettes without breaking eggs, and you can't have cheerful fires without using coal or wood pretty freely.

Don't let your wife pledge your credit beyond what is necessary and reasonable. She must learn to cut her coat according to her cloth.

Don't think your wife cares for nothing but money. Money doesn't make happiness, but the lack of it can cause a good deal of misery. When your views and hers on money matters conflict, think what a lot she has to do with her share of the family income.

Don't dole out money for your wife's personal use in sixpences on the ground that, as you pay the bills, she can't really require any money. It is hateful to a woman to have to ask for what should be hers by right.

Don't try to live on too big a scale, and don't let your wife persuade you into it against your better judgment.

Don't take a bigger house than you need just for show. You will find it will need more servants, more furniture, more everything, and you will have to scrape to keep up appearances, instead of being comfortable on a less expensive plane.

Don't live on the edge of your income while leading your wife to suppose that you have plenty of money. If she doesn't know the financial situation, she can't act for the best.

Don't spend the best years of your life in thinking of nothing but money-getting.   Enjoy your life to the full with your wife and children, and relegate money-getting to its proper place —necessarily an important one, but not the only thing to be thought of.

Don't let all the economising be on your wife's side.   Perhaps you could do with a little less tobacco, or fewer cigars or cigarettes, or fewer taxis, if you tried.

Don't persuade your wife to hand over to you for investment any money she may have of her own.   Your intentions are the best in the world, but she will find it difficult not to hold you responsible if the investments prove to be unsatisfactory.   Keep clear of her private income.

Don't get her to put her private money into your bank, "as it is the same thing." Let her keep a separate bank account, and then she will know just where she is, and be able to do as she likes with her own.

Don't ever let yourself think that marriage has spoilt your career—that if you had had no wife and children to provide for, you could have done so differently.   Think rather of the happiness you would have missed that has been yours all these years.

Don't be ungracious when your wife lavishes her private money on you.   It takes a strong man to receive favours readily; if you really care for your wife, you will let her do things for you occasionally, and accept her offerings graciously.

V.—HOUSEHOLD MATTERS.

Don't interfere with your wife's household management. Nothing upsets servants more than interference in matters of detail from the master of the house.

Don't forget to be master in your own house, but see that your wife is mistress.

Don't sneer at your wife's cookery, or bridge-playing, or singing, or, in fact, at anything that she does. If you do, you may raise an animosity you cannot easily allay.

Don't make up your mind to a mother-in-law difficulty. If you take her the right way, you will probably find your mother-in-law not only a charming woman, but one of your best friends.

Don't domineer over the servants. Unwilling service is never good, and a kind word or a pleasant smile will do wonders in the way of saving your wife from being harassed.

Don't run away with the idea that there is nothing to do in a house, and that your wife should therefore never be busy or tired. You work for a few hours at the office, and come right away from it until next day; but a woman's work is never done until bedtime, and then she lies awake and thinks of something she has left undone.

Don't grumble day after day at your wife's untidiness if you happen to be a methodical man. It will be much easier, and will save friction, if you quietly put away the things she leaves lying about. Her untidiness may be a constitutional defect, and, if so, no amount of grumbling will cure it.

Don't argue that no wife need be dull at home because there's always plenty to do. Of course there is; it is just the deadly monotony of it that some natures can't stand.

Don't let your wife feel that there isn't a corner of the house she can call her own. If there is only one "den," let her have half of it, or at least a roll-top desk or a bureau for her special use.

Don't be unsympathetic if your wife's worries seem to you to be trivial. You haven't tried to run a house with tiresome servants and ailing children, and you don't realise what a strain it is at times, and how molehills become mountains, because there are so many of them piled on to each other. You can soon sweep all the trouble away with a little kindly sympathy, or you can make it worse by refusing to see that there *is* any trouble.

Don't think your business worries are ever so much more important. The others are *her* business worries, and just as real to her as yours are to you.

Don't be persuaded, even if you are unfortunately childless, or if your children have married, to give up your home and live in hotels or boarding-houses. All the mechanical conveniences and perfect service won't make up for the loss of your own home. With all its imperfections, it is *yours*, and you can do as you like in it.

Don't be afraid of lending a hand in the house during a temporary servant difficulty, or if you keep no servant. It will do you no harm at all to learn to light a fire or clean a pair of boots, and be sure your wife will have to do plenty of things that *she* is unaccustomed to.

Don't let your wife become merely a domestic machine. If she doesn't want to broaden her horizon, see that you do it for her. But probably she only wants a little encouragement to lift herself out of the everlasting groove.

Don't show your worst side at home. You need to be well thought of by your wife and children even more than by strangers. You spend hours only with outsiders, but you spend your life with your family, and it depends on your conduct whether they make you happy or wretched. Let them have the benefit of your best qualities.

Don't be too didactic in your home. Your wife is not to be treated as a schoolgirl to have the law laid down by you.

Don't forget that character is more important than genius. If your wife is a true woman, don't worry about the rest.

Don't omit to cultivate a sense of humour. It will carry you safely past many a danger-signal in the home.

VI.—RECREATION AND HOLIDAYS.

Don't selfishly refuse to go out in the evening because you have been amongst other people all day. Remember that your wife hasn't, and a change is good for her.

Don't grudge an occasional evening at the theatre. If you spring it on her as a pleasant surprise, your wife will be all the more delighted.

Don't spend night after night at your club, leaving your wife alone to count the hours until your return.

Don't say she needn't stay up for you. You know quite well that she can't sleep until you are safe at home.

Don't insist on her always being home when you come in. She will like to be there to receive you as often as she can, but if you try to make a rule of it, she will consider it a grievance.

Don't take it for granted that your wife has too much to attend to now there are children to be able to go out with you as she used to do in the earlier days of your life together. Ask her; not perfunctorily, but as if you really want her, and she will generally manage to go.

Don't spring it on your wife five minutes before it is time to start that you are going to the other end of Europe, and would like her to go too. It is all very well to say that it doesn't take long to pack a couple of bags, but sometimes the things are not ready for packing. Besides, your wife has to make arrangements about the house and children which can't always be made at a moment's notice.

Don't think that you have of necessity done with walking or cycling tours now you are married, as you can't leave your wife and go away with your old chum.   Why not take *her?* If you will moderate your ardour, and be content to walk fifteen miles a day instead of twenty, and to carry a slightly larger knapsack (you'll never feel the difference), you and your wife can have the most delightful walking tours together. Or if she cycles, and you will think less of the miles you cover than the charming villages you investigate, you will not need a better chum than she can be.

Don't refuse to play tennis or croquet or billiards with your wife because it is "not worth while" to play games

with a woman.   If she plays badly,
show her how to improve.   She certainly won't play better by being left
out of the game altogether.

Don't tell your wife she is wasting
her time if she plays games occasionally while you are at the office.   It is
the best way to keep her fit, and she
needs a change from the monotony of
the house.

Don't say it is no fun to go out
cycling with your wife because she
can't "scorch."   It will do you no
harm to ride more slowly than usual,
and your company will give her a great
deal of pleasure.   Her "going slow"
is one of the secrets of her chances of
longer life.   Take her with you, and
you will avoid that overtaxing of the

arteries which leads to premature old age.

Don't be nervous about your wife. She can take care of herself much better than you imagine, and she hates you to be fussy.

Don't settle down into an "old married man" while you are still in the prime of life. Take your wife out and about; give parties; visit your friends; and you will keep much younger than if you settle into the smoking-jacket and slippers habit.

Don't say your wife wastes time in reading, even if she reads only fiction. Help her to choose *good* fiction, and let her forget her little worries for an hour occasionally in reading of the lives of others. But, above all things, don't put on the schoolmaster air. She'll never stand that. Rather let her pick her reading for herself.

Don't discourage her if she wants to take up serious reading, even if *you* are not interested in it. Tastes differ, and you needn't call her a blue-stocking because she prefers not to be an ignoramus.

Don't say that other women find fancy needlework a sufficient relaxation. If your wife *doesn't*, why should she waste her time on that instead of going out or doing things that she *does* find recreative?

Don't say it will be holiday enough to stay at home, and spend time on your hobby instead of going to town every day for business. Remember that your wife gets no change that way (except a little extra trouble in house-keeping), and that she needs one quite as much as you do.

Don't rush off on a Continental tour, and come back worn out to be nursed up by your wife. That sort of holiday is worse than useless. Go abroad if you like, but don't spend all your time rushing from place to place sight-seeing.

Don't take a house for your summer holiday, unless your family is so large that you are obliged to. It is no holiday for your wife to have to do her housekeeping—and probably under less convenient conditions—in another

town or village.   If you must do it
for the sake of the children, take her
away to a boarding-house or hotel at
another time to give her a complete
holiday.

Don't insist on giving holidays to
the servants during *your* holiday on the
ground that your wife can "manage"
at the seaside.   You are not the only
person to be considered, and it's no
holiday for her to be tied to the children day in and day out while you go
golfing or fishing.   Probably *she* would
like to golf or fish as well if she got
the chance.

Don't growl every time your wife
invites anyone to the house.   It takes
quite half her pleasure away to know
that you think it's a "nuisance"

having people about. It's bad for you too; nothing is more insidious and more ageing than the hermit habit.

Don't omit to learn to dance as soon as you get married, if your education has been neglected before. Your wife will lose half her pleasures if you can't dance.

VII.—HEALTH.

Don't be impatient if your wife has a headache, or neuralgia, or other ailment. Just because *your* health is perfect, you need not be unsympathetic. But, on the other hand—

Don't pet your wife when her little finger aches until she imagines herself a martyr to ill-health, when there is really nothing the matter with her.

Don't encourage her to be hysterical. You need not be unkind, but you can firmly refuse to pity her.

Don't let your wife become deadly ill before you insist on her seeing a doctor. Some women imagine they are ill, but others never mention it until they are at the last gasp, and *their* husbands should keep their eyes open.

Don't stubbornly refuse to put on your overcoat on a threatening morning, and then when, after getting wet through on the way to the station and sitting in your wet clothes, you develop a bad cold, take it out of your wife by being crotchety and irritable.

Don't insist on your cold dip when you don't feel fit, and then go about all day feeling shivery and miserable.

Don't shut all the windows on the ground that you can't stand draughts, and then complain of a headache.

Don't be too sensitive about your personal appearance to wear glasses if your sight requires them, and if your nose is not the right shape for pince-nez, be satisfied to wear spectacles.

Don't be continually worrying about your health. If you really feel ill, or suspect that anything is wrong, consult a doctor, instead of causing your wife untold anxiety by throwing out vague suggestions as to what "may" be the matter with you.

Don't sit up after midnight regularly, and then get up at the last minute next morning because you don't feel very fit. Get a proper night's rest.

Don't burn the candle at both ends, either as regards work or play. You won't be able to stand it for long.

VIII.—DRESS.

Don't grudge your wife a new dress because *you* haven't noticed that she needs one. You don't know how much trouble she has taken to try and appear —to other people—as if she *didn't* need one; but *she* knows.

Don't argue that a new hat isn't necessary because there is nothing visibly wrong with the one she is wearing. You have probably forgotten that this is its third season, but *she* hasn't.

Don't forget to buy your wife a pair of gloves occasionally. She will always be pleased to have them.

Don't insist on wearing your hair or your moustache in a style you know she hates. Just try it another way to please her.

Don't persist in wearing that very disreputable coat when some rather "starchy" people are coming to tea. If your wearing it makes your wife feel uncomfortable, it won't do you any harm to change it, even if you do think it a bore.

Don't growl when your wife asks you to fasten her dress up the back. You know you consider it a very becoming dress, and it would be spoilt by fastening in front.

Don't dress carelessly when you are past your first youth. All the more reason to make yourself look as nice as possible to counteract the effect of advancing years.

Don't be so absent-minded as to dress yourself "anyhow." Perhaps in the rush to get you off in time for your train, your wife may not notice that you are wearing odd socks; but she will be very uncomfortably conscious of it when she sees you again in the evening, and wonders how many people have happened to observe it during the day. She does her best, but you can't expect her actually to dress you.

Don't refuse to listen to your wife's suggestions on matters of dress. Sometimes women know what suits men better than the men themselves.

Don't try to dress your wife in the fashions of ten years ago. Some men can never like anything newer than that; but a woman does not want to look as if she came out of the ark.

Don't, if your wife is obviously cut out for a "one-piece" collarless dress and a floppy hat, persuade her to wear a "neat" black coat and skirt, high linen collars, and sailor hat, to please your ideas of decorum. She doesn't want to dress like a nursery governess.

Don't take so little interest in your wife's dress that she might as well wear a piece of old sacking as far as you are concerned. It is very discouraging to a woman to find that her husband neither knows nor cares how she dresses.

IX.—HOBBIES.

Don't spend all your money on the garden because that is *your* hobby, and leave none for the house if that happens to be your wife's hobby.

Don't omit to have a hobby of some kind. It will take you out of your wife's way when she is busy or you are cross, and you will feel a different man in half an hour.

Don't separate your pursuits from your wife's more than is necessary. Do your gardening together; work, talk, and plan together, and you will become truer comrades every year.

Don't say a married woman doesn't want to go back to school because your wife wishes to attend language classes or lectures, or to take lessons in singing or dancing. Let her do any or all of these things, and be thankful she finds so much to interest her. She will be a much brighter companion than the stick-at-home wife.

Don't give up cricket, or football, or tennis, or rowing, or whatever outdoor sport you have been accustomed to, just because you are married. Athletics will keep you from becoming flabby.

Of course, if you can get all the exercise you need in a game which your wife can share, so much the better; if not, she is not so selfish as to wish to deprive you of healthy recreation. But remember your responsibilities. Don't overdo it.

Don't expect to have a hobby in which you get the enjoyment while your wife does the hard work. If you profess to like gardening, don't tie up a rose here and there while your wife does all the hard weeding; if poultry-keeping is your hobby, don't expect her to do all the feeding, and the letting out and in of the birds; if photography, don't confine *your* work to the taking of snapshots, leaving her to do the developing and printing while you take the credit.

Don't leave your wife to clean and put away all the tools you use in gardening or carpentering. The workman should care for his own tools.

Don't "put your foot down" if your wife wants to join some society of which you don't approve. Produce your arguments; then, if she fails to find them convincing, let her be an "ist" or an "anti" to her heart's content. She really has as much right to her own opinions as you have, and there is no cause for quarrel.

Don't try to control your wife's church-going or non-church-going tendencies. The question is for her alone to decide, and you should leave her entirely free, whatever your own views may be.

Don't let any hobby so overmaster you that you spend every minute on it when you are at home, especially if it be something in which your wife can take no part. Leave *some* time to devote to her.

Don't, if music be your hobby, practise the violin, 'cello, flute, trombone, or whatever musical instrument you happen to fancy, in the drawing-room for many hours a day. Your wife may also be fond of music, and it is not fair to victimise her to this extent. She won't be able to concentrate on a book while her ear is tortured by false notes. Do your real "practising" up at the top of the house, and play for her pleasure in the drawing-room.

Don't forget to use a reasonable amount of caution should your hobby be one that may be dangerous. Your wife doesn't want you to be "funky," but she has a right to expect you not to take undue risks in your motor-car, bicycle, or flying-machine.

X.—FOOD.

Don't keep up a continual grumble at meal-times, until your wife begins to think she can never please you. She will leave off trying after a while, and your last state will be worse than your first.

Don't be too exacting about your food. If you can't afford an accomplished cook, don't demand elaborate dishes. If you do, it will mean either that your wife will spend most of her time on them, and sit down hot and tired, and perhaps cross, or the cook will spoil them; and in either case there is likely to be discord.

Don't come in at any odd time, and expect to find your dinner done to a turn. If it was ready at the time you *said* you were coming, it can't be quite as nice an hour or two later. Your home is neither a club nor an hotel.

Don't get up too late to eat a decent breakfast before starting out for your day's work. It is bad for you to go without, and will worry your wife.

Don't insist on eating indigestible things because you like them, and then blame your wife's cookery when your liver makes itself felt.

Don't let your wife feel that your dinner is the be-all and end-all of your existence.   Enjoy your food by all means, but don't make a fetish of it.

Don't refuse to eat cold meat at luncheon once in a way if you are home to that meal.   Unless you keep a large staff or domestics, or unless your small staff or your wife is very much overworked and "rushed," you can't always have a hot meal both at midday and in the evening.

Don't insist on having gorgonzola or other strong-smelling cheese on the table or the sideboard twice a day when you know the odour makes your wife feel ill. After all, it is a small thing to forgo in comparison with your wife's comfort.

Don't begin to talk of anything unpleasant while at table. Finish your meal first, and try to banish all worrying thoughts during its progress; otherwise, not only your meal but your wife's will be badly digested.

XI.—CHILDREN.

Don't say anything to your children that may tend in any way to lower their estimation of their mother.

Don't let your wife devote herself so exclusively to the children that you are left out in the cold. She doesn't put you there on purpose, but you must show her that you are still her husband and lover, and expect to be treated as such.

Don't think it a nuisance when your boys or girls want your help in their studies. Give it to them pleasantly if you are able to do it at all; if not, say so.

Don't always say, "Ask your mother," when *you* don't want to be bothered. It is conceivable that *she* doesn't, either.

Don't say, "That's not in my line," when your wife asks your advice about the children. It *ought* to be in your line.

Don't say always that you are too tired to play with your children. They want to feel that they have a father as well as a mother.

Don't forget to set an example to your children of being thoughtful for their mother. They will soon learn to save her in all sorts of little ways if they see that *you* always do it.

Don't be unreasonable in your demands on your wife's time during the child-rearing years. If you join her in her hours with the children, you will find added joys in your life, and will not miss her exclusive attentions to you.

Don't leave to your wife everything in connection with the education and upbringing of the children. Discuss all points of difficulty with her, and come to an agreement as to the best way to act under given circumstances.

Don't let your children fear you. Love, not fear, is the key to their characters.

Don't be a wet blanket. In many households all the light-hearted laughter and chatter ceases automatically as soon as father's step is heard. It might have been turned off at the tap, so sudden is the silence. This is all wrong. Your children should feel that you delight in their pleasure.

Don't stick too closely to the old adage that "Children should be seen and not heard." Of course, you must guard against their making nuisances of themselves, especially before visitors. They must learn not to come into the limelight too much, but you don't want to stifle self-expression. Encourage them to speak freely of their ideas.

DON'TS
FOR WIVES

PREFACE

Art is a hard mistress, and there is no art quite so hard as that of being a wife.

So many women exhaust their artistic power in getting married, which is, after all, a comparatively easy business. It takes a perfect artist to remain married – married in the perfect sense of the term; but most of us have to be content to muddle through.

Imagine a girl called upon without a single lesson to produce a tune – a lot of tunes – in fact, one never-ending succession of harmonies – from the most difficult instrument in the world. Note that the instrument not only gets grumpy in cold weather and skittish in the spring – not only slacks or breaks its strings with every change of temperature – but becomes tempestuous over a tight shoe, broody over an out-of-date egg, and cross, sulky, or mirthful for reasons that no sane woman can understand.

That is what the average wife has to reckon with; and if she intends to play the game – humiliating as some may think it – HE will loom largely on the horizon all her life.

I hope she may find it worthwhile to take a few hints from an old hand.

BLANCHE EBBUTT.

DON'TS FOR WIVES

I.—PERSONALITIES.

DON'T think that there is any satisfactory substitute for love between husband and wife. Respect and esteem make a good foundation, but they won't do alone.

Don't be surprised, if you have married for money, or position, or fame, that you get *only* money, or position, or fame; love cannot be bought.

Don't think that, because you have married for love, you can never know a moment's unhappiness. Life is not a bed of roses, but love will help to extract the thorns.

Don't expect life to be all sunshine. Besides, if there are no clouds, you will lose the opportunity of showing your husband what a good chum you can be.

Don't look at the black side of the cloud. It is only a shadow cast by the silver lining.

Don't lose heart when life seems hard. Look forward to the corner you are bound to turn soon, and point it out to your husband.

Don't moralise by way of winning back the love that seems to be waning. Make yourself extra charming and arrange delicious dinners which include all your husband's favourite dishes.

Don't put showy qualities before honesty and uprightness in your husband.

Don't despise sound common sense because he doesn't indulge in brilliant inspirations.

Don't expect your husband to have all the feminine virtues as well as all the masculine ones. There would be nothing left for *you* if your other half were such a paragon.

Don't be troubled because your husband is not an Adonis. Beauty is only skin deep and the cleverest men are rarely the handsomest, judged by ordinary standards.

Don't worry about little faults in your husband which merely amused you in your lover. If they were not important then, they are not important now. Besides, what about yours?

Don't put on airs with your husband. If you can't be natural with him, you shouldn't have married him.

Don't expect your husband to be an angel. You would get very tired of him if he were.

Don't boast of your husband's money or birth or cleverness to your friends. It is nearly as bad as boasting of your own.

Don't tell all your women friends of your husband's faults, but—

Don't din his perfections into the ears of every woman you meet. Be satisfied to enjoy them.

Don't interpret too literally the 'obey' of the Marriage Service. Your husband has no right to control your individuality.

Don't be discontented and think your husband not 'manly' because he happens to be short and thin, and not very strong. Manliness is not a purely physical quality.

Don't take your husband at his own valuation, but at yours. He may be unduly modest, or just a little too cocksure.

Don't expect a man to see everything

from a woman's point of view. Try to put yourself in his place for a change.

Don't advise your husband on subjects of which you are, if anything, rather more ignorant than he.

Don't try to model your husband on some other woman's husband. Let him be himself and make the best of him.

Don't let your husband feel that you are a 'dear little woman', but no good intellectually. If you find yourself getting stale, wake up your brain. Let there be nothing your husband can talk about that you will be unable to understand.

Don't profess to care nothing about politics. Any man who is worth his salt does care, and many men learn to despise women as a whole because their wives take such an unintelligent attitude.

Don't set your husband up on a pedestal and then cry when you find that he is only an ordinary man, after all.

Don't be talked down by your husband when you want to express your views on any subject. You have a right to be heard.

Don't be rude to people whom you dislike, or your husband will have just cause to be ashamed of you. Politeness costs nothing.

Don't expect to know your husband inside and out within a month of marriage. For a long time you will be making discoveries; file them for future reference.

Don't vegetate as you grow older if you happen to live in the country. Some women are like cows, but there is really no need to stagnate. Keep both brain and body on the move.

Don't consent to be treated as a child who cannot be expected to take any responsibility. Insist on hearing bad news as well as good. You did not marry your husband to be wrapped in cotton wool and put away in a glass case; you married him to be the partner of his joys and sorrows.

Don't omit to pay your husband an occasional compliment. If he looks nice as he comes in dressed for the opera, tell him so. If he has been successful with his chickens, or his garden, or his photography, compliment him on his results. Don't let him have to fall back on self-esteem all the while for want of a little well-directed praise.

Don't pose as a helpless creature who can do nothing for herself; don't drag your husband away from his office to see you across a street; don't profess to be unable to understand Bradshaw, or to take a journey alone. It is true that the weak, clinging wife is often a favourite, but she is equally often a nuisance.

Don't live on top of a spiritual mountain. Try to be

"a creature
Not too bright and good,
For human nature's daily food,"

As Wordsworth has it.

Don't forget to wish your husband good-morning when he sets off to the office. He will feel the lack of your good-bye kiss all day.

Don't brood; that way madness lies. Don't hesitate, if you catch yourself brooding, to 'take a day off' in the best way you can. Go out and gossip with your friend; get to a theatre where there is a play that will make you laugh; or try a concert or a cinema show – anything that will take you out of yourself. Take the brooding habit in time before it gets too strong a hold of you.

Don't stop at that. Half the brooding and half the ill-humour in the world are due to foolish feeding. The woman who broods probably does not trouble about the meals when her husband is away – doesn't have a decent repast at midday, but some bread and butter, or pastries and a cup of tea; or perhaps she eats too much meat.   Three, or even two, meat meals a day tend to make the world look very black to the middle aged. The ever-flowing teapot is as bad.

II.—HOW TO AVOID DISCORD.

Don't expect to drop into matrimonial harmony with the end of the honey-moon; you have not thoroughly learned to know each other's foibles by that time.

Don't expect all the love to be on his

side. It will wear thin for lack of support if you do.

Don't quarrel with your husband. Remember it takes two to make a quarrel; don't you be one of them. Lovers' quarrels may be all very well, but matrimonial doses are apt to leave a bitter flavour behind. The quarrels of spouses are not always the renewal of love.

Don't say, 'I told you so,' to your husband, however much you feel tempted to. It does no good, and he will be grateful to you for *not* saying it.

Don't expect your husband to make *you* happy while you are simply a passive agent. Do your best to make *him* happy and you will find happiness yourself.

Don't nag your husband. If he won't carry out your wishes for love of you, he certainly won't because you nag him.

Don't sulk with your husband. If he has annoyed you about something, 'get it off your chest.' A sulky wife is as bad as a termagant.

Don't tread on your husband's (metaphorical) pet corns. There are plenty of other people who will do that. *You* needn't help.

Don't think you can each go your own way and be as happy as if you pulled in double harness. In all important matters you want to pull together.

Don't expect all the 'give' to be on his side, and all the 'take' on yours.

Don't argue with a stubborn husband. Drop the matter before argument leads to temper. You can generally gain your point in some other way.

Don't 'manage' your husband too visibly. Of course, he may require the most careful management, but you don't want your friends to think of him as a hen-pecked husband. Above all, never let him think you manage him.

Don't wash your dirty linen in public, or even before your most intimate friends. If there are certain disagreeable matters to discuss, take care to discuss them in complete privacy.

Don't go to sleep feeling cross with your husband. If he has annoyed you during the evening, forgive him and close your eyes at peace with him. 'Let not the sun go down upon your wrath' is a very good motto.

Don't return to an old grievance. Once the matter has been thrashed out, let it be forgotten, or at least never allude to it again.

Don't be too proud to seek a reconciliation if you have unhappily quarrelled with your husband. Never mind if you think he was to blame—give him half a chance, and he will probably own up to it; but he may not care to take the first step, lest he be repulsed.

Don't refuse to give way about trifles. When a principle is at stake, it is a different matter, but most matrimonial differences arise from trifles.

Don't say bitter things when you are angry. They not only sting at the time, but they eat their way in and are remembered long after *you* have forgotten them.

Don't keep your sweetest smiles and your best manners for outsiders; let your husband come first.

Don't believe that marriage is a lottery over which you have no control. If you and your husband have both married for love, the lottery is really a 'dead cert'.

Don't attempt to dictate to your husband on any subject. He won't stand it, and there will be trouble. But—

Don't let him dictate to you. Always respond to reasonable persuasion, but let him see that, although you are willing to be led, you are not to be driven.

Don't cease to be lovers because you are married. There is no need for the honeymoon to come to an end while you live.

Don't let your husband feel that you are always criticising everything he does. Leave the role of critic to others. This does not mean that you are to give no friendly criticism. There is a happy medium between constant carping and fulsome flattery which you should seek.

Don't snub your husband. Nothing is more unpleasant for lookers-on than to hear a snub administered by a wife, and it is more than unpleasant for the husband; it is degrading.

Don't ever seem to join forces with those who criticise your husband, even in the length of his moustache or the cut of his hair. He is more sensitive to his little vanities than in his big exploits. The great man will be modest enough about his world-shaking inventions; but if you jibe at the colour of his eyes, you have him on the raw.

Don't forget that you and your husband are a partnership. If he thinks his partner is against him, to whom can he look for sympathy? If YOU join in the world's opposition, he may feel that he is a very Ishmael, and become one, in truth.

III.—HABITS.

Don't be everlastingly trying to change your husband's habits, unless they are *very* bad ones. Take him as you find him, and leave him at peace.

Don't grumble because his idea of work differs from yours. If he works hard at anything, let him do it in his own way, and be satisfied.

Don't grudge your husband his little luxuries—his cigarette, or his pipes, or his books. Who has a better right to them than the man who earns them?

Don't try to wean him from any pet hobby he may have because his things are always about, or because it is such a messy occupation. Let him be as messy as he likes in his own home—only give him plenty of space for his fads, and he won't want to carry them into the living rooms; in fact he would much rather not, lest sacrilegious hands should touch his treasures.

Don't hesitate to inconvenience yourself to give him a den all his own. He's really a good fellow, and a lot of his worries will melt away if he has a place to himself for a while. When he is out, the den will be yours.

Don't say you can't allow smoking in your drawing room, or else don't expect your husband to sit in it. Let his home be Liberty Hall in every respect.

Don't claim to read all your husband's correspondence. Probably he would not have the slightest objection to your doing so if you did not make a point of it.

Don't let your husband expect to read all *your* correspondence as a matter of course. Each should respect the other's privacy.

Don't check your husband's high spirits. Let him sing at the top of his voice in the bathroom, or whistle out of tune on the stairs, and be thankful for a cheerful man about the house.

Don't become a mere echo of your husband. If you never hold an opinion of your own about anything, life will be dreadfully colourless for both of you, and there will be nothing to talk about. Remember that variety is the spice of life, and that the sweetest of echoes is apt to become monotonous.

Don't let your husband sharpen lead pencils all over your drawing-room carpet. He will be none the happier for it, and the carpet will suffer as well as the maid's temper. He doesn't do it out of pure cussedness; it is mere thoughtlessness, and a little instruction will induce him to use the hearth or the waste-paper basket. But don't 'row' him; be good-natured about it. After all, most husbands are only grown-up children in such matters.

Don't encourage your husband to drop, when alone with you, the little courtesies he would show to other women. You are not the *least* important of women to him.

Don't spend half the morning in bed because there is "nothing to get up for."

The day is not long enough for all the things you might do if you liked.

Don't let your husband make you selfish, and don't you make him selfish. If there is one specially comfortable chair that you both like, don't let him always put you into it, and don't persuade him always to sit in it himself. Turn and turn about is a very good rule.

Don't open the door for yourself when your husband is present. He would open it for a lady guest, let him open it for you. Besides, your boys will not learn the little courtesies that count nearly so well by precept as by example.

Don't work yourself into a fever every time your husband omits to turn up at the expected time. He is in all probability neither run over by a motor-car, nor robbed and murdered on his way home, nor lying in a lonely land with a sprained ankle, nor in any other of the terrible predicaments your imagination pictures. Probably he stopped at the bookstall to buy an evening paper, and so missed his train. So don't greet him hysterically when he *does* arrive.

Don't think it beneath you to put your husband's slippers ready for him. On a cold evening, especially, it makes all the difference to his comfort if the soles are warmed through.

IV.—FINANCIAL MATTERS.

Don't think money makes happiness. It helps to procure comfort, but true happiness lies deeper than that.

Don't be satisfied to let your husband work overtime to earn money for frocks for you. Manage with fewer frocks.

Don't get into debt if you can possibly help it. You don't want to carry a load around on your own mind, nor to worry your husband with it.

Don't spend every penny you get, unless it is so little that you absolutely must. Try to put by for the proverbial "rainy day."

Don't expect to begin where your

parents left off. A little struggle in your early married life won't hurt you.

Don't spend your life keeping up appearances. Why should you buy expensive furniture for the benefit of your neighbours if you haven't a balance at the bank?

Don't entrench on your little capital every time you think you would like something which you haven't got. You won't find it so easy to replace these sums as your necessary expenses grow.

Don't have any secrets from your husband in financial matters. Complete confidence is best.

Don't let him have any financial secrets from you. You are partners, and you have as much right to know what is the balance at the bank as he has.

Don't spend all the best years of your life pinching and saving unnecessarily, until you are too old to get any pleasure out of your money.

Don't pile up money for your children. Give them the best education possible, and let them make their own way.

Don't urge your husband to save enough money to "retire." His retirement may very likely shorten his life by depriving him of its chief interest.

Don't exercise your passion for economy on your husband's linen. Don't expect him to wear his shirts and collars twice because the laundry bill is so high, and don't grudge him a couple of handkerchiefs a day. If necessary, you can wash these yourself. Anyhow, rather economise on your own or the household washing.

Don't consent to let your husband pay all the wages and tradesmen's books and your dress bills, and then say there is nothing for which you need money. Some wives have to ask their husbands for every halfpenny stamp they want; not because money is scarce, but because their husbands like to feel their power. Don't let yours begin it.

Don't forget that you have a right to some money to spend as you like; you earn it as wife, and mother, and house-keeper. Very likely you will spend it on the house or the children when you get it; but that doesn't matter—it is yours to spend as you like.

Don't impose on your husband's good nature. Because he is 'such a dear,' and will give you anything you like to ask for, don't take advantage and ask for something unreasonable.

Don't grudge the trouble of keeping accounts. It is worth while knowing what becomes of your money.

Don't hesitate to plan out large expenditures with your husband. Usually a woman is very good at small economics, but often a man has a better grip of essentials in spending large amounts.

Don't run up big bills at a number of shops and then find it necessary to go to your husband to help you out. Try to know where you are all the time.

Don't confuse stinginess with economy. You can be careful without being mean.

Don't object to your husband's life insurance. He will die none the sooner because his life is insured, and if you should unfortunately have to end your life without him, it may be a great help to you.

V.—EVENINGS AT HOME.

Don't be out if you can help it when your husband gets home after his day's work.

Don't let him have to search the house for you. Listen for his latch-key and meet him on the threshold.

Don't omit the kiss of greeting. It cheers a man when he is tired to feel that his wife is glad to see him home.

Don't greet him at the door with a catalogue of the dreadful crimes committed by servants during the day.

Don't think your husband horrid if he seems a bit irritable; probably he has had a very trying day, and his nerves are overwrought.

Don't forget if he is 'nervy' to watch if the tea habit is getting too strong in him. Nerves are often due to too much tea as to too much worry.

Don't bother your husband with a stream of senseless chatter if you can see that he is very fatigued. Help him to the tit-bits at dinner; modulate your voice; don't remark on his silence. If you have any cheery little anecdote to relate, tell it with quiet humour, and by-and-by he will respond. But if you tackle him in the wrong way, the two of you will spend a miserable evening.

Don't 'fuss' your husband. Mistaken attentions often annoy a man dreadfully. If he comes home late after a busy day, and has a quiet little supper alone he doesn't want you to jump up like a Jack-in-the-box with 'would you like more pepper, darling?' and present him with the cruet from the opposite end of the table, when he already has one in front of him. See that everything is conveniently placed for him and then leave the man alone until he has fed. Let him feel your sympathetic presence near him, but occupy yourself in reading or doing needlework; anyhow, don't 'fuss' him.

Don't spend all your time with the children, and leave none over for your husband. You can have them during the day; it is your husband's turn when he comes home in the evening.

Don't nauseate your husband with talking 'baby' *all* the time. As baby's father, he will stand a good deal of it, but remember that there are other interests in the world.

Don't get the idea that all your husband wants is a housekeeper, or a decorative head of the table. He wants a companion and when he is at home he doesn't want you to be always somewhere else.

Don't choose the very time your husband is at home to 'see about' all sorts of things in other parts of the house. Sit with him by the fire; smoke with him if it pleases you and him; read or be read to; sing or play cards with him, or chat with him about anything that interests him.   It is your business to keep him amused in the evening.

Don't say you don't want to be bothered with business details.   By all means encourage your husband to put business worries behind him, but sometimes he can do that best by telling them to you.

Don't tell your husband of every petty annoyance and pin-prick you have suffered from during the day, but *do* tell him your real troubles; he expects to share them, and his advice may help you.   In any case, his sympathy will halve the trouble.

Don't be shy of showing your love. Don't expect him to take it for granted. A playful caress as you pass his chair, an unexpected touch on the shoulder, makes all the difference between merely *knowing* that you care for him and actually *feeling* it.

Don't expect your husband to want to spend evenings at home if you don't make home the most comfortable place. Don't stuff your drawing room with priceless knick knacks that he will knock over when he stretches out his hand for an ash tray. Don't have chairs that look nice but are not comfortable to sit in, nor cushions that may only be looked at. It is a mistake to suppose that a man likes best the home of the 'pattern' housekeeper. He doesn't; it makes him want to kick things about.

Don't sit and yawn while your husband is smoking his last pipe, or finishing his novel or his game of patience. And don't mutely reproach him by going to sleep in an armchair. If you are too tired to stay up decently, go to bed, but don't try to hurry your husband off before he is ready.

Don't refuse to see your husband's jokes. They may be pretty poor ones, but it won't hurt you to smile at them.

Don't be too serious and heavy at home. Make things bright for your husband.

Don't grumble because your husband insists on wearing an old coat in the house. He wears it because it is the most comfortable garment he possesses, and home is the place for comfort.

Don't think it too much trouble to sing or play in an evening with your husband as sole audience. You couldn't have a more indulgent or appreciative one, as a general rule.

VI.—JEALOUSY

Don't be jealous of your husband's bachelor friends. Let him camp out with them for an occasional weekend if he wants to. He will come back all the fresher, and full of appreciation of his home.

Don't be jealous of your husband's acquaintance with other women. You don't want him to think you are the nicest woman in the world because he never sees any others, but because he sees plenty, and still feels that you are the only one in the world for him. Have nice girls about the house pretty frequently.

Don't give up all your men friends when you marry, and don't expect your husband to cease to take an interest in his women friends. Ask both to your home, and welcome them equally.

Don't try to excite your husband's jealousy by flirting with other men. You may succeed better than you want to. It is like playing with tigers and edged tools and volcanoes all in one.

Don't try too hard to regulate your husband's pleasures, and don't be jealous if they don't *always* include you.

Don't be jealous of your husband's club. If you are, he will go all the more. If you are perfectly willing for him to go as often as he likes, he would probably rather take you to the theatre.

Don't object to your husband cycling in to the country just because *you* don't cycle. If you can't, or mustn't, or don't want to, that's no reason for cutting off one of *his* chief pleasures.

Don't be jealous of your girl when she grows up because you are afraid you will have to take a back seat. Remain your daughter's companion, interested in all that interests her, and nobody will dream of drawing comparisons. She will never 'put your nose out of joint.'

Don't be jealous of your daughter's influence with her father. It won't undermine *yours* if you play your part properly. There is nothing more charming than the fellowship of a man and his budding daughter.

Don't be jealous of your husband's work. If he is any good, he is bound to be interested in it, and, after all, he is working for *you*.

Don't fill your heart with vain imaginings if your husband's business takes him away from you for weeks at a time. He is a good fellow, or you would not have married him. You must trust him; it is the essence of married life. But also—

Don't let him coop you up while he is away. You must live your life; you

cannot vegetate. He must trust you.
Any other attitude is an insult.

Don't forget the mountain and the
molehill. Don't insist that your molehill
is a mountain if you suspect your
husband of flirting. There is no more
certain way of making it into one. Your
husband is only human, and if he is to
be hanged, he would probably rather be
hanged for a sheep than a lamb.

Don't be jealous, anyway. It belittles
you, puts you at a disadvantage, and, if
your husband thinks about it, is apt to
make   him   unbearably   conceited.
Nothing makes you look old and worn
sooner than jealousy, and nothing
makes you more ridiculous.

VII.—RECREATION

Don't be afraid of being thought unfashionable if you go out with your husband; if you love each other, you will want to take your pleasures together as far as possible. On the other hand—

Don't object to your husband spending Saturday afternoons playing cricket because you can't play too. You can watch, or you can enjoy some pleasure that is not in his line, and it is advisable for him to have outdoor recreation.

Don't scoff at your husband as 'too old for tennis.' As long as he can play the game he is not too old for it.

Don't forget the anniversary of your wedding. Keep it up. The little celebration will draw you closer together year by year.

Don't think it is childish to celebrate birthdays. Your husband may not say anything, but he will carry an inward grievance if you forget the date. You need not buy expensive gifts, but let there be *something* special for him on that day. Ask his best friend to a nice little dinner, or arrange to dine in town together, and go to a theatre.

Don't refuse to take an interest in your husband's hobbies, but don't let him leave all the tiresome part of the work to you. If he loves to keep chickens, let him get up half an hour earlier in the morning to feed them. On the other hand, don't grudge a little help, and always be ready to sympathise about the broody hen or the fighting cockerel.

Don't encourage your husband to save money by pottering around at home during his holidays. It will do you both far more good to get a complete change of air and scene.

Don't insist on rushing about the Continent to see cities during your husband's summer holiday if he feels that a quiet rest by the sea, with a good golf-links handy, will be better for him. Never mind if you do get enough of the country; *he* doesn't, and you can run over to Paris for a week at some other time without wearing out your husband's nerves when they should be resting.

Don't say you can't go abroad if your husband wants to, because you don't like the Channel-crossing, and you hate foreign ways and foreign food. Subordinate your wishes to his for once, and you'll be surprised to find how much pleasure you pick up by the way.

Don't expect your husband always to share *your* recreations while you refuse to share his. If you like concerts best, and he prefers plays, let each sacrifice to the other in turn, and you will be surprised to find how your tastes become more catholic as time goes on.

Don't be afraid to rough it now and again with your husband as a companion. If he feels that he would like a week's walking tour with you as a chum, don't object that it may rain, or that you haven't a suitable dress, or that you can't manage for a week with nothing in the way of luggage except a nightdress and a tooth-brush. Enter into the spirit of the thing, and you'll get quite as much fun out of it as he will, and be happier than if he accompanied you to some fashionable resort where you would need to dress three or four times a day.

Don't take any notice of people who tell you constantly that a wife's place is in her husband's home, darning socks and stockings as women did in the good old days. You can darn all the socks and stockings there are to be darned, and you can be at home whenever your husband is, and very often when he is not, and yet leave plenty of time for going out.

Don't omit to fill your life with plenty of outside interests. If you sing, join a choral society; belong to a lecture or literary society; keep up your French and your music; visit your friends, and invite them to visit you. Nothing induces dullness, and even illness, so easily as lack of congenial occupation. You will come back to your husband with a bright face instead of a doleful one.

Don't get into the habit of staying indoors because there is nothing particular to go out for. Make an object if you have not got one: take the dog for a run on the common; walk to a shop two miles away to match some wool—anything to prevent the stay-at-home habit from growing upon you.

Don't say you can't go out with your husband because you can't leave the children. Make arrangements that will enable you to leave them in satisfactory hands.

Don't refuse to run up to town for a couple of days, when your husband has to go on business, on the plea that you have 'nothing to wear.' Go in what you've got, and have a good time.

Don't object to your husband getting a motor-bicycle; merely insist that he shall buy a side-car for you at the same time.

Don't say that golf is a selfish game, and a married man ought to give it up.

You learn to play, and then join a mixed club; your husband will be only too delighted to have you with him. But don't make up your mind that you could never like the game until you've tried it. Never mind if you don't become a crack player; the main thing is to derive pleasure from community of interest.

VIII.—FOOD

Don't forget to 'feed the brute' well. Much depends on the state of his digestion.

Don't talk to your husband about anything of a worrying nature until he has finished his evening meal.

Don't buy expensive food, and have it

ruined in the cooking. If your cook isn't up to French dishes, be satisfied with English ones cooked to perfection.

Don't let your cook persist in frying steak when your husband likes it grilled, or in serving his eggs hard-boiled when he likes them milky.

Don't be afraid of cold meat. A few cookery lessons, or even a good cookery-book, with the use of a little intelligence, will make you mistress of delicious ways of serving up 'left overs'. Some men like it, but cold mutton has wrecked many happy homes.

Don't persist in having mushrooms on the table when you know they always make your husband ill. They may be *your* favourite dish, but is it worth it?

Don't give your husband burnt porridge. It is not enough to supply a double saucepan; you must see that it is regularly used.

Don't keep a servant who can't be punctual with meals. Nothing upsets a hungry man's temper more than being kept waiting for his dinner.

Don't let breakfast be a 'snatch' meal. Your husband often does the best part of his day's work on it, and the engine can't work if you don't stoke it properly.

Don't be careless about the way in which meals are served when you and your husband are alone. Dainty surroundings do much to make eating an agreeable process, instead of a mere means of keeping oneself alive.

Don't despise trifles. When two people make a home, the happiness of that home depends on trifles. For instance—

Don't despise the domestic potato. There are a hundred appetising ways of cooking it; but unless you take it firmly in hand, it will arrive at table with the consistency of half-melted ice—mushy without, stony within. The boiled potato is the rock on which many a happy home barque has foundered.

Don't give your husband stale bread if he prefers it new, nor new bread if it produces indigestion. Exercise a little thought in the matter.

Don't let your husband off the carving of the joint because he doesn't like doing it or does it badly. You have plenty of other things to do, and, besides, you don't want to show him up as a helpless man.

IX.—DRESS.

Don't take your husband on a laborious shopping expedition, and expect him to remain good-tempered throughout. If you want his advice on some special dress purchase, arrange to attend to that first, and then let him off. Men, as a rule, hate indiscriminate shopping.

Don't let your husband get into the habit of never noticing when you wear a new gown. Some men would be none the wiser if their wives wore sackcloth and ashes, but it is very discouraging to the wives.

Don't let your husband feel that it is a matter of indifference to you if he wears his socks wrong side out, or odd boots on his feet. Some men are absent-minded enough even for this; and if they can't keep a valet, their wives should see that they dress properly.

Don't let your husband wear a violet tie with grass-green socks. If he is unhappily devoid of the colour sense, he must be forcibly restrained, but—

Don't be sarcastic about your husband's taste in dress. Be gently persuasive and train his sense of fitness.

Don't impose your ideas on your husband in matters of individual taste so long as his style is not bad. He has a right to his own views.

Don't be induced to wear tailor-mades if they don't suit you just because your husband notices how well they suit so many other women. Probably you know best what suits *you*. But, on the other hand—

Don't reject your husband's advice on matters of dress without good reason. Many men have excellent taste and original ideas on the subject.

Don't think your husband extravagant because he pays more for his clothes than your brothers or your friends' husbands do. He pays for the cut as well as the material, and think how you would like to have your gowns made by a third-rate dressmaker.

Don't run away with the idea that it doesn't take a man as long to dress as a woman, and then be surprised that he keeps you waiting. Valet him yourself if you want him to be ready in time.

Don't dress badly, even if your allowance is small. If you can't have new gowns with every fleeting change of fashion, never have them made in an extreme style, so that they may not be too accurately dated. Let them be of good material, dainty, and well cut; there is nothing gained by being dowdy.

Don't allow yourself to get into the habit of dressing carelessly when there is 'only' your husband to see you. Depend upon it he has no use for faded tea-gowns and badly dressed hair, and he abhors the sight of curling pins as much as other men do. He is a man after all, and if his wife does not take the trouble to charm him, there are plenty of other women who will.

X.—ENTERTAINING.

Don't refuse to entertain your husband's friends on the ground that it is a 'bother'. Nothing pains a man more than finding only a cold welcome when he brings home a chum.

Don't be slavishly wedded to the dinner for dinner principle in entertaining. If you are, you must, of course, refuse all invitations which you cannot return in kind. But, after all, your friends are not really starving, and if some other form of entertaining suits you better, why be so hide-bound? Friendship is not a matter of bargaining.

Don't worry about getting into the 'very best' Society—with a big capital 'S'—afforded by your town or suburb. If the aristocratic inhabitants don't call on you, or the wealthy ones think you are not rich enough, it is not a matter to trouble you. A few friends are worth a host of acquaintances, and most of the really nice people will find you out.

Don't let visitors who are staying in the house feel themselves in the way. Give them the run of the place; don't shut them up in state in the drawing room.

Don't try to 'amuse' your guests every minute of the day. If they feel thoroughly at home, the amusement will come naturally. Don't forget to have books in every room.

Don't refuse to entertain at all because you can't do it on the same scale as your neighbours. The 'jolly little party' is generally preferred to the starchy reception.

Don't refuse to adapt yourself to the style of entertaining which is first favourite in your locality. If you are thrown amongst a non musical set of people, it is not the least use inviting them to be miserable at a musical evening. If, on the other hand, your lot is cast amongst a set that despises cards, it is hopeless to issue invitations for a bridge-party.

Don't say you can't give progressive bridge-parties because you can't afford to buy expensive prizes. Make up for it in the care with which you select them; let them be good of their kind and unpretentious, and you will find the lucky winners quite as pleased with your prize as an elaborate one won elsewhere, which cost as many pounds as yours cost shillings.

Don't feel worried because you can't afford to offer your friends a champagne supper. They can be just as jolly on claret-cup, and will think none the less of you for keeping within your means.

Don't in any case try to entertain in a way that is beyond your means just because other people do it.

XI.—HOUSEHOLD MANAGE-
MENT.

Don't sneer at your mother's old-fash-
ioned ways. They suited your father
well enough, and perhaps she can give
you points.

Don't sneer at your mother in law's
old fashioned ways; you may hurt your
husband as well as his mother.

Don't think anything too much
trouble to do for your husband's
comfort; remember he is occupied all
day in working for *you*. Don't be afraid
of thinking and planning and working
for *him*.

Don't think your household gods of
more importance than your husband's

comfort. Don't for instance refuse to give him a bedroom fire in cold weather because it makes 'too much dust.'

Don't keep the house so tidy that your husband is afraid to leave a newspaper lying about. Few men have such a sense of order as most women have, and they are naturally more careless at home than at the office. But what does it matter when you really come to think of it?

Don't quarrel with your husband's relatives. If you can't get on with them, don't ask them to visit you, but persuade your husband to visit *them* occasionally. As a rule, however, a little tact and patience will carry you over the thin ice.

Don't allow outsiders to interfere in your household management. Even mothers should lie low, but—

Don't refuse to listen to good advice from people of experience, and act upon it if you can.

Don't get angry if your husband says that he never now tastes cake like that his mother used to make. Write and ask her for the recipe.

Don't become too stereotyped to try new methods that may be better than the old ones.

Don't let the house get stuffy by sitting with closed windows. Keep the air moving, and let your husband come home to a healthy atmosphere in more than one sense.

Don't let fashionable wives persuade you to give up your home and live in hotels or boarding-houses. It may be less troublesome for you, but it is also less comfortable, and infinitely less pleasing to the average man. If you've got a home of your own, stick to it and be happy in it. You don't want to live your lives in public.

Don't forget your poorer neighbours. If every family that had enough to eat kept an eye on even one family that hadn't, there would be much less misery in the country.

Don't omit to oil the wheels of the domestic machinery so that they don't annoy your husband by running badly. If you can't keep your servants in a good temper, change them. Don't make things uncomfortable by scolding them in your husbands' presence for sins of omission and commission. In fact, keep the machinery in the background as much as possible, letting him see only the results. But—

Don't forget that your husband is your chum and will be delighted to be called upon in an emergency. Your young husband will like to save you by lighting the early morning fire when you are 'in a hole.'

Don't have a 'spring cleaning' any oftener than your special nature renders absolutely necessary. Some women have at least four every year. When you do have one, don't upset the whole house at once. Men hate to find a place in disorder, and if you take one room at a time, your husband need know very little about it except when workmen are required.

Don't have your husband's den turned upside down once a week, and everything put back into a different place. When the necessary amount of sweeping and dusting has been done, replace everything as nearly as possible in the position in which he left it, even if it is not quite 'tidy.' You can be tidy in your own part of the house to make up for it.

Don't be afraid of soiling your hands if it be necessary. There is nothing undignified about housework, and if circumstances make it necessary or advisable for you to do it, do it to the very best of your ability. Besides, it's a good thing to be able to feel that you never expect anything of your servants that you couldn't do for yourself if it were expedient.

Don't permit yourself to forget for a single instant that nothing is more annoying to a tired man than the sight of a half-finished laundry work. The remotest hint in your home of a 'washing day' is like a red rag to a bull.

Don't get up at six every morning, and don't expect your husband to do it either, to see if the maids are stirring. When you engage a servant, explain that you expect her to rely upon herself for getting up to time. Send her to bed in good time. Give her a reliable clock and let her take the responsibility.

Don't be a household martyr. Some wives are never happy unless they are miserable, but their husbands don't appreciate this peculiar trait. The woeful smile is most exasperating.

Don't let your servants use paraffin for fire-lighting purposes, nor leave a newspaper fastened up in front of the fireplace to 'draw up' the fire. If you do, they will probably have your house set on fire some time or other.

Don't say it's a waste of time to make marmalade at home when you can get it better made from the stores. Your husband and children never like *any* so well as yours, and it is worth the trouble of making to see how they enjoy eating it.

Don't omit to learn how to put on a bandage. You will be very lucky if you get through your married life without having to do it for some member of the family, and the right way is so much better than the wrong one.

Don't forget to reduce the housework to a minimum by abolishing all *unnecessary* polishing of metal, washing of curtains and sweeping of carpets.

Don't swathe all your chairs and couches in covers while they look nice and fresh. Time enough for that when they become shabby. Furniture wrappers banish the 'homey' feeling.

Don't arrange for the chimney sweep to come on the day your husband happens to be staying at home. He won't like either the sooty smell or the subsequent upset for cleaning purposes.

XII.—CHILDREN.

Don't omit to take your husband into your confidence on matters connected with the training of the children. Let him bring his wits to bear on the problems that are troubling you.

Don't let your husband become merely your children's father after the arrival of the first baby. You can give him an extra share of love in that capacity, but he won't want to be any the less your husband and chum.

Don't cease to call him by his

Christian name and begin to address him always in the children's presence and out of it as 'Father' or 'daddy.'

Don't go to either extreme with regard to the amount of the children's society that you give their father. Let 'enough, but not too much' be your motto.

Don't think your baby is as interesting to everyone else as he is to you. It is quite natural for *you* to think that there never was such a wonderful baby before, but other people are apt to smile at each other or become horribly bored if you can talk of nothing else.

Don't say your husband 'looks silly' with a baby in his arms. Let him realise that the youngster is partly his, and that there is nothing derogatory to his dignity in handling him.

Don't give baby the same name as his father, and then have to talk of 'Big John' and 'Little John', or of 'Old John' and 'Young John'. Call your husband always by his own name, and let your boys have names of their own too.

Don't grudge the years you spend on child-bearing and child-rearing. Remember you are training future citizens, and it is the most important mission in the world.

© Copyright A&C Black Publishers Limited, 2008

Originally published 1913

Republished 2007 by A & C Black Publishers Limited

36 Soho Square, London W1D 3QY

www.acblack.com

ISBN 978-1-4351-1341-1

10 9 8 7 6 5 4 3 2 1

A CIP catalogue record for this book is available from the British Library.

Printed by WKT Company Ltd, China